*If you are reading this, you have found
The Message at the perfect time.*

*It is as much energetic conversation
as it is written word.*

Experience it.

Take your time.

Allow The Message to unfold within you.

Copyright © 2020, Julianna Lovett

All rights reserved. No part of this publication may be reproduced, distributed or transmitted in any form or by any means without permission of the publisher, except in the case of brief quotations referencing the body of work and in accordance with copyright law.

ISBN - 978-1-913479-59-6 (Print)

Book Design: bodhi-design.co.uk

First edition published in 2020
That Guy's House
20-22 Wenlock Road
London
England
N1 7GU

You Are Here   7
   There is no way out, only the Way

PART I

A Call To Self-Realization   15
   You are more than you allow

An Invitation To Live Your Truth   19
   Allow your life to happen

Forget Everything You Know   31
   You are on this Earth to learn

PART II

You Are Your Own Guide   37
   There is no hierarchy

Remember Who You Are   41
   A guided visualization

It's Time To Take Responsibility   49
   Accepting your empowerment

PART III

Empowered Co-Creation   55
   Finding the balance in giving and receiving

Living With Passion   65
   When everything connects

How Life Works   69
   There are no rules

God Is An Idea   77
   Connecting beyond words

PART IV

You Are An Equal Part Of The Whole   85
   A call to live with truth and courage

STEP ONTO THE PATH
Embracing An Unconventional Path To Self-Realization   95

Author's Note   99

The Message

You Are Here

There is no way out, only the Way

This is a message for dreamers
    for those who know that there is Life
        with a capital 'L'

Life to be lived
Life to be known
A true Life
    that's all your own

◎

Hope is a word that
    harms
It isn't necessary
There is only
    Is

There is no struggle
There is no striving
You're already
    there
And guess what?
So
   is
      everyone
            else

◎

Oh, beautiful ones
The days pass
    the years pass
  yet your beauty never fades

Your value is
   eternal
Your wisdom is
   ageless
Have no fear of *anything* ever fading

You can be nothing but what you are
   now
        forever
            always

◎

You have the right as an eternal creature
   to wind your way through space and time
      through experience after experience
     absorbing each one
        fulfilling your quest for Self-Realization:
                self-understanding

The Message

All paths lead to the Source
You are everywhere
       and nowhere
   eternal in your being
   finite in your pursuit

Your focus on each moment
   creates your experience
Every moment
   is in every moment

◎

Stop trying to control
   what
      when
         where
            how much

Remove "control" from your vocabulary
Allow it only as a concept
     a memory
         an experience
   to wash out of you
     so that you may be free
       to exist

Feel the resistance within your physical being
Feel the parts that resist your entirety
       the vastness which lies beyond and within you
         in an incomprehensible space and time

◎

You Are Here

From the conscious pinpoint that holds you in your vehicle:
                                                          your body
    allow yourself to be whole and vibrant
                neutral

Let your vehicle's size grow
        or shrink
    into the perfect form for its maximum mobility

Choose anew
    to allow
Allow your highest knowing
      your highest expression of your Self
    to be the commander of your vessel

Awaken now
    your understanding of the treasure trove of memories and knowledge
    that reside within your whole being

Attune your brain and neural pathways
           the emotional
                           the intangible
                                              the tangible

Allow every part to attune to your particular frequency
            audio
            sensory
            tactile
            visual

Taste
        touch
            feel
                discover the way your frequency feels
Learn to recognize your unique channel within All That Is

◎

The Message

You are a receptor
        and a transmitter

The energy flows
    in and out
              up and down
                        side to side
                                    all around

                    There is no way out

                    There is only the Way

PART I

Part I

A Call To Self-Realization

You are more than you allow

The times you live in require you to wake up from your indulgent dream
and live more purposefully through your heart and your soul
to leave behind the games of your mind and your ego
and live purposefully with love and light

You have evolved into a being of great power
yet you do not understand your power

◎

That part of you which is blocked from remembering
the source from where you came
has also grown stronger

Therefore, the more powerful you get
    the more powerful your block gets
This block enslaves you
    in the reality that you can see
It limits your experience and understanding
    of the beauty and the flow of the life force
        in its many forms
It limits your access to the full right of your beingness:
        the right to be connected to All That Is

◎

You do harm to yourselves and everything around you
    without a second thought
    without remembering that you are also
        the blades of grass you walk on
        the air you breathe
        the water you drink
        the water you pollute

You are connected beyond the earth plane
    and beyond what you can see
        to life that exists way beyond your comprehension

This means that you are also a part of
    every soul that you kill

◎

I come to you today to speak of a way through the block
        through the confusion

As a human being you are capable of so much more
    than what you allow yourself to be

It is my desire (for those who are willing)
    that you walk a path of
        light
            joy
                peace
                    tranquility
                        passion
                            power
                                and co-creation

This message is for everyone waking up on the path of
    Light
        Love
            Power
                Creation
to experience mindful connectedness with who they really are
                          with the world around them
                                and with All That Is

                This is for you who are brave enough
                    to allow yourselves to be
                    more than you can conceive

Part I

An Invitation To Live Your Truth

Allow your life to happen

You've been wandering through life on autopilot
    separated from your true nature
    distant from who you really are

Listen now
Find your way back to yourself
              to your Source
              to that of which you are a part:
                           All That Is

◎

First
You must recognize the divinity within yourself
    and everyone else on the planet
If you look deep into another's eyes you will see
    a spark of love and connection that is for you
It is there to show you that you are a part of
    everyone
           and everything

You have the ability to see the emotion in everything
                                      in *every* living being
        even one who is filled with hate or poison
                like a rattlesnake or a murderer
Hate and venom are but a shadow for their true nature

Shadows, too, are a part of what you are a part of:
        the Divine Form that connects All That Is

Once you see this within yourself you will be amazed
    by how easy it is to spot in everything
        and everyone around you

For you cannot see in others
    what you cannot see in yourself

So, recognize the beauty
        the goodness
        the wholeness
    that lives within you
Then you will be able to recognize it
    in all living things around you

◎

Next
You must fight!
    Fight to keep alive that spark of Truth within you

Once you see it, do not let the light burn out
    Tend to that fire
Feed that fire so that it grows and grows
    until finally it fills you
    until it's detectable by anyone around you

Eventually
    your light will be unmistakable
        even to a pilot flying tens of thousands of feet above the earth

Shine
    Glow
        Grow
Fill the world around you
   with the light that is within you
   with the fire of the Truth that burns deep within you

Hold this responsibility
   sacred
Make it a priority over everything else in your life
     even the responsibility you feel towards
        your children
        your partner
        your aging parents

For if you are not true to yourself
   it is most difficult to be of service to others

You must always
   first be in service to yourself
         your body
         your spirit
         your soul

◎

Next
You must follow the path
   which becomes illuminated before you

Once you've recognized this beauty
     and this Truth within you
   and you've found the fire that lights the way
     you will see clearly all that is before you

With your impeccable vision
   you must follow the path which is yours

Follow your path with focus
   but not with blinders
Stay open and receptive to all that you see around you
   so that, moment by moment
     you are making the choices that are best for you
         that are meant for you

Live your life with your passion and your fire ignited and burning
     fueled by the Truth of who you are

Seek that same Truth in all others
    without bias
    without discrimination

Never discriminate with your clear and beautiful sight

Share unconditionally
     without thought of receiving
   that which is yours to give
   that which comes from the fire within you

◎

Sing when you must sing
   Be silent when you must be silent

Practice
      Practice
         Practice
Learn to listen to the voice within you
   that voice which is the true voice
   the most consciously connected voice

Listen to the source of who you are
       to All That Is

Listen and be guided
    by the wisdom that resides within you
Do not be swayed by anyone
        even those with the best of intentions
            your priest
            your rabbi
            your political leader
            your boss
            your partner
            your parents
            your children

They do not know you and cannot guide you on *your* path
    in a way that is better for you
        than following your inner knowingness

Even if you are in conflict with one whom you deem to be wise and kind
    you must respectfully acknowledge your connection
        while still moving forward on *your* path
            in the manner you know to be true for you

When you act out of love and self-direction
    your energy is not projected onto others in a way that is harmful to them
It is their responsibility how they perceive it

You will not contribute to any misunderstanding
        or breach of trust and connectedness
    if you proceed in this way
            in your integrity

◎

None of this means to show disregard for other living creatures

In all ways, your path must be in harmony
    with the paths of your fellow travelers
Because you now know the truth
    that their paths are also a part of your larger path
You are all a part of All That Is

It's like being a single blood cell within the body
You must be in harmony with the rest of the cells
    which are in harmony with the veins
        which are in harmony with the skin
            which are in harmony with the organs...

You must respectfully find the balance and harmony
    between your existence and all that is around you
Because you are now aware
    that everything is a part of you

Your heart
        and the way you understand your heart
    must open
        for you to live in this manner

You must give and receive fully
    removing fear
        fear that comes from the lies you were told
        and the misconception you have about the way life is

For there is no heartache or pain imposed by others
    or imposed by having an open heart

In fact, the more you close and protect your heart
    the more pain you experience
    the more pain you hold onto

When you let the natural flow happen
    all the emotions can come in and flow out
        in perfect balance and harmony

Therefore, you feel the pain or the disappointment less
    when your heart channel is open
        because then the pain is free to flow out
            and all the other loving things can flow in at the same time

Now you know to approach yourself and your life
    with complete openness and acceptance
        and to allow the flow to move in and out of you

Receive it all and transmute it with your truth
    and your understanding
Then send it back out to all that is around you
      every blade of grass
      every animal
      every person
      every article of clothing
          the air around you
            all the beings
              all that you cannot see with your human eyes

This is what it means to be in the Flow:
                          Take life in
                              process it
                                    then send it back out

Do all of this with an open clear channel for your mind, body and spirit
    striving to eliminate the blocks that keep your Life Force from flowing

For it is your thoughts that create the rocks
    in the middle of the river that you are traveling
        the rocks that stop your raft
            that block you from that free open flow

It is your fear that creates these obstacles
        fear created by your thoughts of all things that are not
            necessary
                    real
                  or true

These obstacles force your mind to focus on them
    diverting your energy toward illusion

Your fear stops the flow
      and your ability to give and receive
           what truly matters

Strive for a fear-free mind and heart
    so that your focus doesn't get caught
        and create a block

Close your eyes and really experience this

When you stop to focus on something
    you literally stop
        instead of noticing it float by you
            as you travel down the river of your life

When you stop
    you start to feel the push of the water damming up
    you are holding on
    you are trying to look too closely at something
        rather than letting it come in and flow through
           along its natural course within your life
This is when you feel the pain
              the aches
              the confusion
              the fear

Take a moment now
    to notice what you feel
It's all for you
    because you are experiencing it

The Message

What do you now know?
    If it's meant for you
        notice it
            let it happen
                        don't block it
    let it move through
        around
            over
        under
      in
Whatever its natural course, just notice it
                allow it

Allow your life to happen and you will be free
    free of so much of what causes you anguish
                stress
                anxiety
                conflict
                pain

Let the energy move through

Notice your life

Flow with your life

Don't try to control *anything*

Trust your inner knowingness
    Trust the fire and the passion within you
And just give!

Give who you are
Give what you have
    in every moment
    in every situation

Don't stop
Don't block
Don't think
    Just do
    Just be

These are some of the keys to living a
   full
      flowing
           stress-free
                  life
Embrace them
Practice them
    Really learn them

Share these keys with others

Read them until you understand

    It's *that* important

Keep trying
If it doesn't make sense at first
    read it again

The Message

Part I

Forget Everything You Know

You are on this Earth to learn

Oh, how beautiful you are when you stand in your power
    and claim your right to co-create
        to co-create *your* life
And in return
    to co-create the form and force of the energy that you are a part of:
                                                    All That Is

You can imagine it as a living, breathing life form
    that encompasses all that your mind can comprehend
        to the farthest reaches
                and then beyond that

Have faith and trust in your connectedness to All That Is
        to all that you can see
           and all that you can't see
    and accept the Truth of that connectedness
        and all of its ramifications

That is all you need to know
The rest is for you to live
    in your power
    in your creation
    in your creativity
        and your passion
        and your emotions
        and all the things that your human body can encompass

◎

First
You must forget what the world has told you
   about who you are
   about who your God is
      and who your God is not

You must forget whoever has wronged you
You must forget the pain and the desire for revenge
   that you felt as a result of those injuries

◎

Next
You must forget the lies that you've been told
   and listen only to the Truth that lives within you

When you read these words
   you must go within yourself
Take 10 deep breaths
     slow and mindful
Fill yourself with the light
   of the highest form of All That Is

Fill yourself with those 10 breaths
        with knowledge that is uniquely yours
        with the Truth of who you are

                Then, you will be ready to receive
                   the message that follows

PART II

PART II

You Are Your Own Guide
There is no hierarchy

As you pursue your mission
      of Self-Realization
   remember that the religions of the world
     have created hierarchies
         that you should now know do not exist for you

You are on this earth to stand in your own integrity
    and to bring into tangible beingness (for your fellow travelers)
      that which you co-create
They are simultaneously sharing their creation
   while mirroring yours back to you

It's as if a light is switched on in your head
     and in your being
  so that you may
          see
            feel
              touch
                  taste
              hear
           smell
    and sense
      all that is here
      all that you are

The first step toward true experience
    is forgetting what you know

Each of you stands as your own guide
      the ruler of your own life
            of your own destiny
You are a co-creator with All That Is

It's like turning the knob on a dimmer switch
As you grow in consciousness
      the light gets brighter and brighter
            until you are standing in your own integrity
                      in your own power
                      in your own fullness of co-creation

Then, you are visible to those who are like you
    and you can see all who share a kindred spirit
And you can work together to make your reality
        and that of everyone around you, more real
                              true
                              honest
                              loving
                              empowered

◎

It is never the intention of All That Is to form a hierarchy over Itself
      or within Itself

There are those who have gone before
There are those that have learned first
    With full willingness, grace and love
        they offer their support to you on your journey

Everyone knows who their people are
    and seeks those who vibrate in harmony with them
All you have to do is contact your inner knowingness
        that connection you have to All That Is

Anyone who has gone before you
        and has the wisdom you seek
  will openly and patiently do so
        from the seen or unseen worlds

Once you fully embrace this power to connect
                this empowered Truth of who you are
    everything that you need to know
        and everything that you need to survive
    is within your grasp

        An important aspect of forgetting
        is to forget all that you have believed
    about how surviving in the current reality works

Part II

Remember Who You Are

A guided visualization

This is an exercise to do before moving on to Part III.
Read the words slowly,
allowing space for contemplation
and new understanding.

Now I ask you to go within
    and to feel what truth feels like in you
It will be slightly different for each of you
    as each of you connects with All That Is
        in your own way
        in your own space

No two parts of the whole are exactly the same

Therefore, your experience within this space
    will be unique

When you go within,
    I want you to feel what *your* connection feels like
Feel what *your* balance is
    what *your* physical weight is in your ideal form

Where does the energy pull you?
    Is it at your heart?
    Is it at your groin?
    Is it at your second or third chakra?
    Is it pulling you up through your crown?
    Is it tugging at your third eye?
  Where are you led?
  Where do you feel?

Now
What do you know?
    What do you know about *your* power of creation?

What is it that *you* do?
        Who is it that *you* are?

It is your right to know this

It is only the block (which is now lifted)
   that keeps you from experiencing this balance
      and this place of creation

Now
You must feel
    and know
    and take the information in
  but not from your conscious mind
     which may have difficulty with the forgetting
        and with this whole new way of understanding
           and relating to All That Is

Rather
   take the wisdom in through the chakra
      or the area of your body
    where you have the strongest connection to this reality
       your heart
       your groin
       your stomach
       your solar plexus
       the top of your head
       your toe
          ...wherever that is for you

The Message

Take it in
Take in the knowingness now
Filter it into your cells
        including the cells of your brain
    and into the electrical currents
      that stimulate your consciousness

Accept who you are *now*
   and how you create
See who you are
       Use all six senses
Use the space of knowingness that surrounds you now
     See it
          Smell it
               Taste it
                    Feel it

Hear the sounds
   Know the thoughts
Say it out loud
   Talk through it
Use all your senses
   What do you smell like?
   What does your power feel like?
              ...taste like?
              ...look like?

How do *you* create?

Use all of your senses

See beyond the images
Move past your clothing
        your skin color
Let your relationships fade away

Ignore the views
          and the images
                    and the idea of you
   that those closest to you
     and farthest from you
have of you

See with your knowingness
     with new eyes
              new ears
                    new taste
                            new touch
                              see
                      feel
              hear
        smell
    taste
know
     …who you really are

Not what your mother thought you were the day you were born

Not how you were raised

Not any previous image that you have of yourself

You will now see who you really are
   and experience full sensory awareness of who you are physically
                                                              mentally
                                                              emotionally
        and how you co-create with All That Is
            in this reality
                    in this life
                            on this plane

Just notice whatever comes first
    the littlest thing
It could be a color
      a smell
        an image

The Message

You might be washing the dishes
You might be taking a walk
You might be sleeping
You might be working with your hands
You might be speaking
You might be listening
You might be loving a single person
     or embracing many

It will be different for
     every
          single
               one of you

Your image is unique to yourself

No one can give this image to you
No one can show you
  because only *you* see you
                  …who you really are

Only *you* can feel your full power

Only *you* can create the way that you create

◎

None of this means that you are alone
   that others cannot see parts of you
      and show you parts of yourself
Every experience helps you turn the dimmer switch up

It also does not mean that others cannot experience you
   through making love
                      through touch
                                through energy
            through conversation
   through love

You are connected to everyone
   and they know you as another part of themselves
But they cannot know
   that part which is totally unique to *you*

Others can only see and experience what you show them
   and then, only what they are able to perceive

It is not your responsibility
     or your concern
   to make anyone understand
     who you are

          It is only your responsibility to be who you really are
             and to create what only you can create

The Message

Part II

It's Time To Take Responsibility
Accepting your empowerment

I have said
    You must forget
        everything you think you know
    You must remember
        who you really are
    You must create
        what only you can create

That brings us to the next step on your path to Self-Realization:
                      empowered co-creation

◎

I say co-creation because you are a part of All That Is
    and there is no way to separate yourself from that

Therefore
    you cannot create alone because you are not separate
        That is the meaning of co-creation

So, from now on, when I speak of creation
    you'll understand that you do it as part of a whole

However, even though you are part of a whole
    only you can create the way that you create
There is no other part within the whole
    that can do what you do
          not what you perceive of as God
              or anything else
              or anyone else

You are your own unique part of the whole

You are the only one that can create what you create

◎

If you haven't already
    you must now take in the truth of your full connection
        Feel it
            Know it
                Touch it
                    Taste it
                        Hear it
Because without the understanding
      and the acknowledgement of your full empowerment
    you will not be able to understand the rest
        You will not be able to continue on this path

The Message

You will be blessed as a part of the whole
    on whatever path you choose
But to travel this self-directed path to Self-Realization
      you must accept the truth of your empowered nature
          and your wholly unique ability
             to create in the way that only you can create

You must accept the responsibility
      and make the commitment to exist in this empowered state
          consciously co-creating

I will explain all as we go along
    but you really can go no further without this acceptance
    and without the full sensory acknowledgement
        of this truth

Now
for those that have made the commitment
        and have accepted the truth
    we move forward into creation

PART III

Part III

Empowered Co-Creation
Finding the balance in giving and receiving

Creation is
    anything that gives form to a thought
                            idea
                            feeling
                            object
                                          ...anything

It is
    giving
            emitting
                    being

◎

Receptivity and reciprocity
   are part of the cycle of creation
One is not more powerful than the other
Both are necessary for the other to exist

Therefore, when you think of creation
    you must also think and experience the qualities of
                                          acceptance
                        receptivity
        flow

Now that you have accepted this
    now that you are in this space
  you can trust that the truth is within you
    trust that you have woken up

There will be times that you will have a hard time
    seeing this true vision of yourself
        (like after a shower, when the mirror gets foggy)
But now that you have done the work to see your true image
    Own it!
    Claim it!

There is no going back

From this point forward there is no other way of being
    or thinking

If you cannot accept that
    if you do not know this to be true
  it would be better for you to stop now

Wherever you are in your thoughts
        your feelings
    in all of your senses
  be with yourself there
    until you are comfortable enough to move on

  That way, you avoid the risk of hurting yourself and those around you
        intentionally or unintentionally

>   Now, back to this business of creating
>   and what I spoke about
>   as the true nature of reciprocity
>   here on the earth plane

◎

When you give
               you receive

When you emit your truth
    you attract what resonates with your truth
        anything from people to money
               all the things that money can and cannot buy, like
                  food
                  shelter
                  clothing
                  travel
                        ...all experiences

So, in your empowered state of being
    in this truth of how the universe works
        that you have now embraced
   your job is to create
        (to give what you uniquely have the power to give)
     and to accept in return
        what others are empowered to give to you

That is your equal exchange
    and it will look different for each of you
For some, it may look like 90% barter, 10% cash
    and it could be exactly the opposite for others

Whatever you need as a result of what you give
        whatever puts back into balance All That Is
   comes to you
All you have to do is accept it
                ...but you have to accept it

If you do not receive, balance is not achieved
    and other things will need to be shifted to create a new balance
Because the nature of All That Is
    is to be in balance

You must receive money
              power
              support
              love (sexual/platonic/spiritual)
Whatever comes to you
    you must receive it

Receiving is the counterbalance
    for that which you have given

The gift or payment that others give to you is all part of the balance
    of them giving
        and then receiving

As you give, you must receive
    As they receive, they must give
As they give, they must receive
    and you must give, and then receive
Do you understand?
    Do you see how this works?
The exchange is necessary for your survival

◎

Each of you
        in your co-creation
    has an innate sense of what your environment should be like

Some are at home near the ocean
    some in the desert
    some in the mountains
    some at sea
    some in the air
    some in the city
    some in the country
    some in a house
    some in an apartment

You must not be distracted by what you see around you
    by what creates balance for another person
  or by someone else's lifestyle

You must never look outside of yourself
    to ask what you need
    or to find *your* true balance
Rather, you must give and receive
Be open to that which is attracted to you
    seeking to provide your balance

◎

The things that you will say "no" to
 situations that you will say "no" to
    people that you will say "no" to
        are those which are not a part of you

Your eye and your mind will see all kinds of things
    that exist to provide balance to other people
        They may look beautiful
        They may taste good
        They may smell good
        They may seem like a good idea for you
But when you are in this new reality
    you will find *your* balance for what you give
        and what you receive
        and it will look different for you than for those around you

Empowered Co-Creation

You will most likely not receive the amount of cash
    that a billionaire receives
You may
        or you may not
But when you go inside of yourself and experience your connectedness
                                        your creation
                                        your empowered beingness
    you will find *your* balance of what you receive for what you give
        and that will change over time

It is not that you are to strive to be poor
                          or hungry
        or to not have nice things
You must simply become aware of
    what being in balance is for *you*
What someone else may have to pay $5,000 for
    you may receive for free

Do you see what I'm saying?

The natural state of All That Is
    is to have balance in *all* things

◎

All that you need comes to you
    to create the balance within your part of All That Is
                and within the whole of All That Is
That is reciprocity

You do not need to go to a job to earn a paycheck
    unless, within your true knowingness you feel that is right for you
And if it is
    you will be balanced
        and content
    because you are creating in your unique way
            Your giving and receiving are in balance

And you must
    ...you *must* understand
        that it will look different for you than for others

For those of you who choose to partner
    when marriage or children are part of your balance
    (a part of your giving and receiving)
    you will find that you are more aware of the balancing that takes place
        in the giving and receiving within those closest relationships

This balance of creating and receiving happens
    within the family dynamic when you are young
  and as you grow older it happens
    within the dynamic of your closest relationships

Always go within yourself to feel the balance
And when you are out of balance you must give and receive
  to put yourself back into balance
        ...however that looks for you

It may be working more hours to receive more money from a paycheck
It may be resting in order to receive energy
It may be being of service to a loved one or a stranger

You must see and experience with all of your senses
    all that is within your immediate reach
  and accept and reject
      and give and receive
    that which your knowingness tells you is right for you
        moment by moment

Empowered Co-Creation

Then you find peace and the flow
      the unencumbered, unrestricted flow of who *you* are
                            of *your* life
                            of *your* beingness
                            of *your* emotions
                            of *your* body
                            of *your* thoughts
                            of *your* soul

            That is survival

            That is creation

            That is beingness

The Message

Part III

Living With Passion
When everything connects

The third component to living in this new way
        is passion

You can understand the meaning of passion
    when you go within yourself and experience a thought
                                      a touch
                                                        a taste
                                                        a sound
                                                        a smell
                                                        a sight
      in such a way that it electrifies the physical body
        and nourishes your spirit
                your consciousness
                your ideas
                your soul
A sound brings you a new idea
Music makes you weep
        When all of your senses are working together
                                                    ...that is passion

Living with Passion

A taste invokes a memory
A memory invokes a smell
    a feeling
    a laugh
A laugh lightens the spirit
 and nourishes the body
The food that you take in
  makes all of your cells sing at a frequency that inspires
   a brush stroke
    a word to a client
     or an idea on the factory floor

◎

Any time that all of your senses
    all of these things
 are working together
   that is passion

Passion, and that sense of connectedness between all parts of your being
 are necessary in order for you to consciously exist in this new reality
  that you are now experiencing

To continue on this path…
To continue living in this way
 all of your senses must be connected and working together
   in a passionate way
  in order for your full power of creation to manifest

◎

Once you have established the pattern of creation within yourself
 it works the same as the law of giving and receiving

You will then attract people, music, things
      ...whatever it is that feeds that connectedness
You will connect with them
   and they will give to you
      and you will receive
   and you will give
      and they will receive
   then they must give
            and so on and so on

Everything flows to you as you pay attention
   and selectively receive and give with your newfound discernment
      and use the filter that you now have in place to only allow in and out
         that which creates harmony and balance
         that which is truly yours to create

◎

Putting blinders up against the distractions
   of what others are giving and receiving
      that is passion

Part III

How Life Works
There are no rules

I spoke about the power that is unrecognized and misinterpreted
    by those who have not gone within
        to find the balance that you now understand

You now know what you need to know in order to experience
    life as you have a right to live it
    life as an empowered co-creator
        as a passionate being in flow with yourself and
                with All That Is

        Now I will discuss more specific things
        that will be useful to those who wish to continue

◎

The larger concerns of others are not your concern
Each individual is responsible for their own destiny
        It is that simple

It appears more complicated when certain individuals
     like presidents
        kings
        rulers
        the wealthy
  use resources to create circumstances for others
        but that is all they are doing
They are creating circumstances that affect you
            or don't affect you

Regardless, the power and the balance of your daily life is always within *you*
    your balance of giving and receiving

All that you need is yours
    All that you have you must give

◎

You may wonder, in a world filled with
  always-on media
  constant electronic interactions
  and so many who don't understand the true nature of survival
     how are you supposed to relate and function?
        Do you watch television?
        Do you eat meat?
        Do you fight for a cause?
        Do you raise a family?
Are there rules?

The answer is
  No
    There are no rules

It is up to each of you individually to decide what is acceptable
     within your range of balance
  and what is appropriate for your creation

Some of you may create as politicians
        as leaders of your communities or the world
    and if you are one of those
        all the same guidance applies

Within your knowingness, you know what you must do
        what it is that you came here to do
    and who it is that you truly are

◎

Each individual is on their own path
    All paths intersect because everyone is part of All That Is

Those who are suffering are part of you
        the depressed
        the hungry
                ...*anyone* who suffers

Those who have murdered are part of everyone
        as are those in charge of a vast percentage of the world's resources

Those who are leaders
    are also a part of you and all the others

At the heart of it all is the basic tenet of
        each individual giving and creating what they have
            and receiving what they need
                in order to achieve balance

I hear a judgmental voice from some of you:
        "But... they have more!"
            they have husbands!"
            they have wives!"
            they have love!"
            they have money!"

Every *they* is another part of *you*

If you feel out of balance, ask yourself:
        "What is it that I need?"
You may only need a one-bedroom home in the middle of the country
    or you may need a 5,000 sq ft penthouse apartment in the city
What do *you* need?

Just because someone else has it
    does not mean that you need it

◎

Once you get to that place of truly knowing your balance
    you will know if you lack
        if you *truly* lack
You may not need an intimate relationship
    or a mortgage like your friends have
A relationship or a house may cause imbalance
        blocking what you know you have to create

When you are in balance, you will be satisfied

It goes back to the first thing you must do
    You must forget
        forget the image that you have of yourself
        forget the image that others have of you

Because in all likelihood you've been living in a way
    other than what you now know is the true way for you to live

So, your ideas of what you must have
      or must not have
    come from a source other than your true nature
You must be open and willing
        to be in balance

You must be open and willing to believe and live the truth
    that comes from deep within you
        even if your partner, your children, your parents
            ...whoever you believe you cannot exist without
        do not accept this truth

You will only be able to move into co-creation and passion
    once you live *your* truth

And you will find that whomever
        or whatever
    must leave your life to create balance
        or must come into your life to maintain balance
    will flow to you and from you
        keeping you in a circle of connectedness
                of knowingness
    as you keep your light shining with your
        passion
            creation
                reciprocity
                    and balance

◎

Be willing
Be demanding
Exist how you know you must exist
    Period

Be willing to exist as you know you must exist
    whatever that means for you

Reject the images
        sounds
        tastes
        feelings
        information
   that try to manipulate you into wanting what others have
     what others don't have
                what others think you should have
     what others think you should not have

Be honest
Be amazed
Be willing to receive your life
        and *only* your life
   not that life, which before this moment, you thought was yours
        and you are guaranteed to have
            passion
                and balance

If you pursue things out of envy
        money
        love
        sex
        ...whatever you desire
   thinking that you will have balance and passion
       you will not find them if you are not living in your integrity:
           in the truth of what you uniquely are here to create

◎

Once you let go of the relationship or the money
       or once you accept them, if meant for you
when they are truly *yours*
   you will have peace
            balance
            passion
     and all of the experiences that go along with that life

But you must first give up
    that which is not truly meant for you

Letting go of what is not meant for you
    is the source of true beingness
            of true living
Doing this is the secret to having the life that you desire
    and only *you* know that secret

You are empowered
Take action now!

It is your right to live a life of balance and passion
      passion being the connection of all of your senses
      balance being the relationship of giving and receiving

Find your place
      within yourself
      within the world around you

Part III

God Is An Idea
Connecting beyond words

What those who can accept must understand at this time
   is the nature of God
        ...the nature of themselves in relation to All That Is

God is an idea
   It is an idea because humans have put a word to it

When human beings started using language
   as a faster way of communicating in this reality
      they lost touch with what is now called the sixth sense

This sixth sense is innately human
   and is equal to smell or touch or sight
It is a means of connecting to and feeling one another
   by way of being part of All That Is
It is intended as a free and open means of communication
   just as sound and touch are

So, from that standpoint
     God is what you perceive God to be
Because by the very nature of putting words around God
   you limit God

God Is An Idea

To dwell upon the idea of God
   is not what was intended

It is words that place your attention on an object
                                      an idea
                                      a thought
                                      a feeling

◎

In your pure form
    when you communicate through that sixth channel of perceiving one another
        (as you would perceive a sensation in your toe or your fingertip)
      you can experience, without interruption or error
          the pure essence of your connection to each other, and to All That Is
              without the limitations of words to diminish your experience
The fewer words you use, the better

The need to be understood is not satisfied by using words
    to tell others about you
        or to persuade others to understand your point of view
In fact, your words limit your communication

This is different than what you've been raised to believe
    but the truth is, when using your words
       as well as the other senses that you are more comfortable using
    you are operating at only 1.2% of what you are capable of
The rest of the communication...
The rest of the knowingness...
The rest of the connection that you feel to yourself
                            to this reality
                            to this earth
                            to one another
                            to All That Is
    comes from this extra sense that, over time,
        you have dulled and denied

◎

If you want someone to understand you
   you must communicate with them without words
You must feel them
You must open yourself and allow them to feel you
                                to sense you
                                to know you

Now, most people are not aware
   that they even communicate on that level
That is not your concern

If you understand at all what I am saying
     if you sense its trueness
     if your knowingness connects with the truth of my words
   then you are to embrace your newfound knowledge
You are to speak less and communicate more

It is not your concern how
     or if
   others receive your communication

Without realizing it
   everyone is emitting who they are
       and it is your job to sense who they are
             to sense the earth
             to sense what's happening around you

If you do this
   you will be living as you are truly meant to live
You will continue to grow in your connection to All That Is
        which is what I believe you strive for

It is only an open channel
        which is not encumbered with your words
    that gives you a pure thought

Words can stifle your communication
Only by going around this lazy form of communication do you truly connect
          (It's not necessarily lazy, but a crutch
        that has been created and handed down to you
          by those who depended upon that crutch themselves)

But, no longer are you dependent upon that crutch
    because now you know the truth:
          You do not utilize the vast majority of your ability
              to sense and communicate

Now, you must quiet the words
          quiet the mind
          quiet your thoughts
Make still your voice
        your body
        your beingness
   in order that you may, with grace, and in light and power
     be present wherever you are
          to transmit who you are and all that is yours to share

You are to open your channel and be filled
    and let your fullness overflow to all around you
                  to the earth beneath you
                  to the objects you touch
                  to the people within your sight
                  to the food that's in your mouth
                  to the air that you breathe

Everything that is touched by the beingness of who you are
    will be blessed when the flow within you is free and full

Then, others will know who you are
    and you can feel that connectedness to yourself
                      to those around you
                      to the Light that you walk within

The Message

Part IV

PART IV

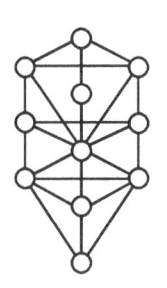

You Are An Equal Part Of The Whole

A call to live with truth and courage

It is time for you to wake up
           to wake up to who you really are
   to get up out of your dream
   to look around you with new eyes
     and see from your heart and from your knowingness
        All That Is

It is your right
It is within you
It is your purpose to live fully and completely
   aware and awake
       connected to All That Is
       connected to all that encompasses your idea of
     God
        Spirit
          All That Is

You are a part
      (an equal part)
   of the whole
None is greater than the other

These constructs and hierarchies that you have built
                        that your ancestors have built
                        that you have been taught
                        that have become part of your reality
   only serve to keep you from being all that you are
       to keep you from being connected to your true Self

Every single one of you has equal access to the Source
   and if you really think about it, you will know this to be true
       beyond a shadow of a doubt
You will feel that this is true

◎

How can it make sense that some who are made exactly like you
   should be in between you and your Source?
How can that make sense to you?

The United States Declaration of Independence talks about equality
   "We hold these truths to be self-evident, that all men are created equal, that they are endowed by their Creator with certain unalienable Rights, that among these are Life, Liberty and the pursuit of Happiness."

Even though the authors' intent was not inclusive
      and the energy of equality has yet to be realized
   this Truth found its way to the planet to serve as a beacon
      while humanity wakes up

These words are true for everyone, regardless of country
   but you choose to allow others to distort them for you
You do not live as though this is Truth

In times of turmoil, many hide behind a flag
     or their beliefs
   which is often easier than standing up for the Truth

But when you start to open your eyes
                        open yourself
                        open your heart
                        open your knowingness
                        open your feelings
   you will see that you are ignoring the Truth
      that all humans are created equal

Think about this
Accept it as Truth
        Then behave as though it is true

Take your power back

You are doing no one
        (including yourself and those that you believe you are helping)
   any favors by giving away your power
                              your knowingness

◎

The religious leaders of this world
    are in fact political leaders

If they look within themselves, they will know this truth
They can find their rightful place
        Everyone has their own place
                They have a place

◎

Your happiness depends on you waking up to yourself
        feeling and acknowledging your connectedness
            your direct, inseverable connectedness
                    to All That Is

Feel that
Know that
>> And behave accordingly

Interact with the rest of humanity and the earth around you
> in accordance with your Truth

Give who you are

Find that place that suits you perfectly

When you choose to follow others
> or do things that are not consistent with who you really are
> you are constantly seeking
>> constantly searching
>>> never at peace

It's like trying to drive a moped in the fast lane of the German autobahn
> or trying to drive a Formula One race car in front of a school
>> Certain things don't fit in certain places

Find where you fit and embrace it
> even if it means that you have to change things in your life
> that you once believed were more important
>> than your true place in this world

◎

Now
    ...now that you've understood and really feel the truth
        there can be no relationship
                no other person
                no other thing
                no amount of money
                no location
                no title
                no status
that is more important to you than
    finding
    embracing
        and being fully present to
        and giving from
            your rightful place

Once you understand *who* you are
        and *what* you are
    there can be no other rightful order for you
        than living your authentic life

Any pain, discomfort or turmoil it causes you
    to shift into that rightful place
        will pale in comparison to the
            joy
                peace
                    satisfaction
                        wholeness
        you will feel once you are in your rightful place

Those things that crumble around you in order for this shift to happen
    will be replaced by wonderfully powerful and supportive things

Your new life will rise up around you
    as you step out to meet it
And the things and people that you leave behind will then be free
    to plant themselves in their rightful place
                    because
        you will not be holding them in a place that is not right for them

This is not some esoteric theory
Thinking logically, if you are in the wrong place
    the people that you hold around you in that space
        must also be in the wrong place in relation to you
So, you are not doing them any favors by staying around
            lingering in the wrong place

That said, your transition must be done with grace and compassion
    holding yourself first, while being mindful
        that not everyone wakes up to themselves at the same time
                          or in the same space

◎

So, you gently transition
    remaining mindful of where each individual is on their own path

This is not to suggest that you divorce your partner
                    abandon your kids
                    never pay them money
                    never provide for them
                    never see certain people again
That is not the intention

The intention is to focus your energy where you have the greatest clarity
    about your rightful place as a part of All That Is
        with grace
                integrity
                        and compassion
Find a harmony with those to whom you have made commitments
    that allows you to live the life you now desire

Live as an example to others for finding *their* own place
    and be unwaveringly supportive of their efforts to do so

Once you understand *your* truth
    it is your responsibility to be generous in assisting others to do the same
        honoring both who they become
            and the space that they determine to be right for them

◎

None of this is easy under the heavy influence of the collective dream
        and its misconceptions
    that have been handed down to you for generations

This goes against what you've been taught
        I realize that
Yet, I'd do you no favors by pretending that what is comfortable for you
            (or what you perceive to be comfortable)
    is right for you

Once you feel even a spark of your connectedness
        a spark of the truth of what I'm saying
    you'll start to feel uncomfortable in places that you once believed
    were the only safe havens for you

And you will be compelled by an inner drive
                              to seek
                        to know
            to remember
    all that is yours

You have my support
        and the support of All That Is
    in your quest for finding your Truth
        and giving to the rest of us (who are a part of you)
            all that you have to give

            We look forward to that blessing
            We are grateful for your courage
            We honor who you really are

STEP ONTO THE PATH

∞

Embracing An Unconventional Path To Self-Realization

The Message is an activation that serves as a launching pad for your lifelong journey of Self discovery, recovery and evolution. The path you walk is up to you.

Everything you need is already within you.

Pay attention to the relationships, work, spiritual traditions or health modalities that you feel drawn to. Find what works and dive in with your full heart. Experience what feels important. Then, when you feel complete, don't be afraid to move on. Attachment and envy are your enemies on this journey. Each soul requires a unique set of experiences to fully activate its true nature. Do your best to avoid becoming distracted by practices that seem to be working for someone else. And do not become discouraged if others appear to be farther ahead.

You are now called inward by your own True Voice - the echo within of All That Is.

Come back to *The Message* with fresh eyes whenever you need inspiration. It's like a compass for your soul. Let the passages provide perspective about where you've been, insight into where you are and guidance for what lies ahead. The evolution of the soul spans lifetimes and it can take moments, years or decades to align with the Truths you seek to master. Remember that there are no rules.

*Where you are and who you are is always perfect,
even when it may not appear to be.*

The course of your soul's unfoldment is yours to chart, but you are not meant to travel it alone.

Visit www.TheMessageBooks.com for guided experiences from the book plus resources and tools to help you navigate the shadowy ravines and glistening peaks along the journey of remembering who you are.

*Leave no stone unturned as you forge your
unconventional path to Self-Realization.*

The Message

Author's Note

In December of 2001 I closed the blackout curtains in a Times Square hotel room and relaxed into my normal meditation routine, stilling my mind and opening my spiritual awareness. I set the intention to connect to the highest knowing within myself and receive guidance for the next phase of my life. In those days I always carried a small tape recorder to capture inspirations, so I clicked it on and started to explore. I expected to tap into ideas for a new project or place to live, but instead I found various aspects of God waiting for me, ready to have a conversation - about everything. It was not unlike the long-forgotten conversations I had with that same Voice Within as a child. It was thrilling, and I went back again and again to connect with my Source, which I call *All That Is* in this book and that others call Allah, Yahweh, Shiva, God, Akal Murat, The Great Spirit, Universe, Oneness and many other names.

The Message is the resulting guide to the Truths contemplated during these meditations.

You may, reasonably, be wondering why I waited until 2020 to share what I learned in 2001. For a long time I asked myself that same question. I came back to the recordings many times over the years, to transcribe them, then to organize the content and find the themes. But every time I started to write the book, my life would take me in another direction and I'd forget about it for a while. What I didn't realize at the time is that I was living the words of *The Message* and forging my own unconventional path to Self-Realization, and had been doing so long before I did my first meditation or knew there even was a path.

Author's Note

My particular journey has taken me from big city to small town living; from a successful career in the entertainment industry to spending 5 years dedicated to my spiritual development and ordination as a Christian Mystic Priest; and then, after a painful break with religion, to owning my own spiritual authority and going back to work as a corporate vice president. Along the way I have been bankrupt and flush, happy and depressed, thin and fat, confused and confident.

But, why tell you about my experience at the end of this book, and why is now the time to publish *The Message*?

The answer to both of these questions is: In the two decades since that day in Times Square I have put the Truths held within *The Message* to the test. *I know* that the guidance is powerful, and that achieving Self Realization did not require me to follow a predetermined path or a specific timeline. I also have cultivated a deeply intimate understanding of the infinite and finite parts of myself and know how to integrate them into what I call a *big little life*. Like everyone, I find it challenging to live up to the Truths outlined in The Message day in and day out, but I also know that I did not have to be perfect or special to be invited into this divine relationship with All That Is. I just have to keep showing up… to opportunities that expand my consciousness and the wisdom they bring…then, to the keyboard, camera or gathering to create a space for you to remember all that you are.

The unprecedented events of 2020 also indicate that the time for *The Message* is now. Our attention is focused as a global community around shared challenges, and people of all backgrounds are feeling a pull inward to define who they are and what kind of world they want to live in. *The Message* is a guide for exactly this type of exploration. It encourages us to remember that we are creators, not minions, with the power to shape our individual and collective experience.

We are beautiful in our power; *The Message* reminds us. And it is time to wake up and reclaim this Truth of who we are. The pressure to conform is massive and everywhere we turn we are told to follow "the rules" if we want to feel safe, loved and accepted. Taking full responsibility for our lives can feel daunting, and the process of getting unconditionally honest about where we are and where we truly want to be can feel isolating. But please know that being the architect of your destiny does not mean that you have to take the journey alone. I invite you to join me in living a big little life, and wish you many unexpected joys as you walk your own unconventional path to Self-Realization.

Julianna

August 18, 2020